# ABUNDANCE
## MADE
# CRYSTAL CLEAR!
*A New Start for a NEW YOU!*

# DAWN CRYSTAL

outskirts
press

Outskirts Press, Inc.
http://www.outskirtspress.com

ISBN: 978-1-9772-4689-9

Cover Photo © 2022 John Andrick. All rights reserved - used with permission.

Outskirts Press and the "OP" logo are trademarks belonging to Outskirts Press, Inc.

PRINTED IN THE UNITED STATES OF AMERICA

# DEDICATION

This book is for all those who want to live lives of abundance. It takes some guidance and an open mind to obtain the possibilities of non-traditional methods, including mine. You'll learn how I have worked with others to remove their blockages on their paths to almost limitless abundance.

# TABLE OF CONTENTS

# Foreword

Dawn is a pioneer of voice-sound-energy relief of pain, anxiety, fatigue. She makes life-enhancing sounds with her voice, a gift she discovered as an adult. She has done this for over 20 years with individuals or groups.

She has been rich and homeless, energetic and tired, and she discovered she had a gift in using her voice to relieve herself and others of troubling conditions, like pain, fear, and fatigue.

She now has a sophisticated website, DawnCrystalHealing.com. Dawn feels a Higher Power has guided her to go Internet, go global. She started from nothing, "heart-guided."

The multitude of testimonials to the effectiveness of her technique demonstrates something beneficial is happening. We know that mind and body are interconnected. Hypnosis and auto-suggestion can produce dramatic changes, including pain and fear relief. Many medical successes are attributed to the "placebo effect," where belief in the likely efficacy helps create a cure. Faith healers have had some surprising results, too.

Some of the testimonials are intriguing on their own.

However it works, these are from witnesses to its effectiveness.

Discussing her techniques with Dawn, I found that her description of moving energy throughout the body and overcoming blockages resembled the techniques I learned years ago of auto-suggestion, self-hypnosis, which produce progressive relaxation. I have first-hand knowledge that such techniques worked for me, including relieving occasional tension headaches and facilitating falling asleep.

A related phenomenon is the effectiveness of affirmations, where positive statements about our desired future states often are followed by what we sought. Whether our minds are affected in a way that helps bring this about, or we influence others by our positive attitude, or something more mystical is going on, many people have received positive results from affirmations, where words affect minds and affect outcomes. Do Dawn's voice-sound sessions tap into something similar?

Those who would like to hear Dawn talk about herself and her techniques are invited to listen to this 25-minute interview done in August 2018, https://www.talkshoe.com/conf/summary/4977560.

I have been pleased to help get Dawn's story into print as her writing coach and editor. Another kind of personal change occurred: her energy and optimism have been infectious!

Douglas Winslow Cooper, Ph.D.
douglas@tingandi.com
WriteYourBookWithMe.com
Walden, NY
Summer 2021

# ACKNOWLEDGMENTS

First, and once again, I thank my coach and editor, Douglas Winslow Cooper, Ph.D., without whom I would never have written this book.

My dog, Hoku (Hawaiian for "star"), brings me daily joy and peace and deserves my gratitude. I can't imagine my life without him.

# Preface
## It Isn't Always Easy

Most people who know me today think I have a charmed life.

They think I have an easy life and that I always have.

The truth is, it may seem that way, and I try to emphasize the positive and radiate positivity, but 2020 and 2021 have been terrible years, and of course, I had a terrible childhood.

My life as a child was the opposite of what I have obtained as an adult. I grew up with hardship that lots of people would find overwhelming. I grew up in a chaotic, dysfunctional family. From day one! I have weathered many storms in my childhood, had no foundation or stability back then, watching my family go down the drain with alcohol and drugs. Teachers in my school were not aware that I had learning disabilities due to my home life. As a teenager without friends, foolishly getting pregnant at a young age, suffering a miscarriage at age 16, yet somehow getting my high school diploma, and even getting through a couple of years of college, paying for it independently.

During high school and college, I worked two or more jobs, supporting myself. As a young adult, I served in law enforcement, hoping to help people with my knowledge, experience, and compassion, knowing how hard some people have to work to get out of the gutter into a more positive place.

I weathered two bad, dysfunctional marriages, ending with no love because I did not know how to love myself. I never knew from birth what love was; I had to learn it much later, on my own. I started a couple of businesses without any training, and they were successful for a while. The miracle occurred when I found God, found Him in me, found my gift.

I had searched for the Divine as a child. I came to look within myself on my journey, leading to much self-discovery, realizing that no material object outside myself nor any human relationship could save me.

I ran from failure into homelessness, and I finally found my gift, my true self as a healer. This revelation healed my life, and now I help others.

In 2020 and 2021, I endured a mysterious poisoning that hit me and my beloved dog, Hoku. We were both at death's door. We had many months of detoxification., spending an astronomical amount of money on medical care. I knew we had to persevere to get cured. Only some medical professionals were of help. My gift guided me in this, totally spot-on, correct.

After many months of this medical ordeal, I have finally started to see the light. I am less tired. The miracle is that my dog and I are feeling much better. I owe it to the Divine within me, which I found when young, which has saved me now.

We all have challenges and obstacles in our lives, but if we go within ourselves and question deeply, we will find the answers and guidance we need. I went from almost giving up to finding the way that was the best answer: not to give up, to keep hope, and to find the true self that will lead to an abundant, healthy life.

Dawn Crystal

DawnCrystalHealing@gmail.com

Maui, Hawaii

Summer 2021

# PROLOGUE
## WHAT IS ABUNDANCE?

Abundance is defined as "more than enough." We need enough. We enjoy having more than enough. We feel freer to share with others "more than enough" to use what we have without worrying that it will run out.

Searching amazon.com for books on "abundance" produced over 10,000 titles, including:

*Abundance: The Future Is Better than You Think,* by Diamandis and Kotler

*The Abundance Book,* by Price

*Simple Abundance: A Daybook of Comfort of Joy,* by Breathnach

*The Abundance Codes: Fifty-Two Codes to Unlock Abundance in Every Area of Your Life,* by Hillyer and Barahona

*Blueprint for Abundance: A Self-Help and Self-Love Guide to Abundance from the Inside Out,* by Virgil

*Abundance for All: The Lightworker's Way to Creating Money and True Wealth*, by Ryan

*Abundance Now: Amplify Your Life and Achieve Prosperity Today*, by Nichols and Switzer

*The Abundance Project: 40 Days to More Wealth, Health, Love, and Happiness*, by Rydall

*Creating Money: Attracting Abundance*, by Roman, Parker, et al.

*The Way of Abundance: a 60-Day Journey into a Deeply Meaningful Life*, by Voskamp

*The Jewel of Abundance: Finding Prosperity through the Ancient Wisdom of Yoga*, by O'Brian and Goldberg

*Imagining Abundance: Fundraising, Philanthropy, and a Spiritual Call to Service*, by Robinson.

From the titles, specific themes emerged: money, wealth, prosperity, health, meaningfulness, love, self-help, self-love, and optimism about the future.

The books' costs ranged from a few dollars or less for some in the Kindle ebook format to $120 for the hardcover version of *The Abundance Codes*. That there are 10,000 such books shows there is a strong demand for such information.

In what follows, I will discuss various aspects of abundance and describe sessions with my clients that helped them live their lives more abundantly by using my sound techniques to remove the energy issues that beset them.

## Chapter 1

CLEARING UPPER LIMITS

"**Whether you think you can, or you think you can't – you're right,**" Henry Ford.

From Shakespeare's *Hamlet*, "Why, then, 'tis none to you, **for there is nothing either good or bad, but thinking makes it so.**"

TOO OFTEN, WE are limited not by the nature of the universe but by our thinking.

Yes, we cannot travel faster than the speed of light, but there is no speed limit to our thoughts.

Yes, we cannot get blood from a turnip, but we can get or give a human transfusion if we need one.

Yes, "there's no such thing as a free lunch," but sometimes snacks are free and can get us through the afternoon.

Make do.

Do without.

Use it up.

Wear it out.

This poem reflects that our ancestors knew how to get the most from very little, how to "squeeze a nickel until the buffalo roars," and we can do so very much more in our age of plenty.

What is holding us back? Usually, our mistaken thoughts about limits to our prosperity and happiness.

What is the solution? Clear these limits as the pioneers removed the trees in the wilderness to make room for their homesteads and families. Break through the glass ceiling to the other side, where your desired outcome awaits you.

Since so many of our limits are mental, it is not surprising that the cure is mental/psychological/spiritual. In the following chapters, you will see examples of individuals who had the limits in their lives removed by my sound-energy technique. Let that encourage you to look into the possibility of using non-traditional approaches to clearing the mental/psychological/spiritual barriers currently limiting you.

So, follow me!

## Chapter 2

# CLEARING PROCRASTINATION

LOTS OF PEOPLE have a procrastination problem. Some of my clients ask for help with this. Usually, they don't know the cause.

For myself, I grew up with learning difficulties, in a dysfunctional family, a chaotic family with screaming siblings, druggies, drunks – made it nearly impossible for me to concentrate—a terrible environment.

My second-grade teacher, Mrs. S., did not know what my problem was. She would scream at me, throw my papers on the floor, and send me to sit in the corner, not allowed to speak. That continued: being bullied in school throughout my early school years increased my difficulty in learning.

My fourth-grade teacher, Miss R., would bring in doughnuts and then charge us kids for them. What a humanitarian! After five days, she cut them into pieces once they were stale and gave them to the more impoverished kids, including me.

Lots of negative energy came my way, with a self-image of being stupid and unworthy. So, I understand people who come from difficult beginnings.

I procrastinated. I would want to try something, but I had no confidence.

Much of my life until adulthood was like this. In my 20s, I held a good-paying job as a marketer for seven years. "Call these companies we do business with and see if they will buy our products."

I did well at this, not being pushy, and my bosses were pleased. My first triumph and my life changed! That was all I needed.

I came out of my shy shell and started to overcome those early traumas.

I'll tell you here the story of one of my clients.

I got called by Sally, recent purchaser of a telesummit program, a woman in her mid-70s, divorced by a husband who abandoned her for a younger woman. He owned his company. He took up with his secretary. He left Sally without support or a job. Even so, Sally dared to buy our Happiness program from a telesummit.

During our phone session, I thanked her for purchasing my program. "What do you want to work on?"

"My rich husband left me. I had grown up in a family that had no communication or love, satisfied just to put food on the table; my Eastern European parents saw life as a struggle.

"I was just kind of there, in the background. English at home was poor, and that hurt my progress in school."

Her childhood was similar to mine, leaving her shy and quiet and failing in her studies because of her home life.

Fortunately, she was good-looking and got some modeling jobs that improved her self-confidence. Even so, she still found it hard to be a self-starter, and she was procrastinating.

Sadly, too, her good looks got her rich men who then had superficial relationships with her.

"Sally, at 70 years young, this is a time for you to discard these old beliefs and find strength in yourself. Now you have the opportunity to make a big change in your life, to find out what your interests are."

"I do like people and animals, and Social Security is not paying enough for the lifestyle to which I became accustomed."

I went into the stages of her life with her, clearing the false beliefs she had absorbed, such as being unworthy. We went from birth to age ten, a slow process, and she would report on her feelings as we were clearing. She told me she felt energy releasing from various areas of her body.

"How are you feeling right now?"

"Wow. I feel happy, lighter, no longer blah. Instead, I am ready to take action."

I knew what she wanted. "You need to find a job."

"There is a humane society that is looking for help, low-pay secretarial work, which would be in an environment I would like, as I love animals."

This was a near-miraculous change in Sally. She had been stuck.

Soon after our session, she did get the job with a boss who admired her abilities and liked her personality.

My life and Sally's were similar in some ways. I could understand her lack of early support, which set her life's tone, presenting a mountain range of obstacles. Yet, both of us have found success amidst the chaos, in occupations that bring us joy, releasing us from dependence on others.

Sally and I both know we are now OK.

# Chapter 3

## CLEARING DOUBTS

**MY WHOLE LIFE** has been one big doubt while growing up without any positive reinforcement. I was just winging it, on my own. I had no advisors or helpers in my dysfunctional family. I watched members of my family kill themselves with drugs and alcohol.

I worried about what to wear to school that would not get me ridiculed.

I had two failed marriages, and these made me doubt myself. My healing journey in Maui had the surprise of the arrival of my healing gift, and I doubted it at first. Why did it work? Would it help others? Were they helped? They seemed to be grateful, and they even paid me, so I began to believe they were helped.

Positive outcomes finally convinced me that I was doing what was good and proper. I no longer have those doubts. I have found my Soul's calling.

"Yvonne" and I worked together for almost two years, on and off, and she follows me on the telesummits. She usually buys a session associated with my talks, a personal session.

When I call her, often she is nervous, not at all grounded. Our sessions start with efforts to relieve her, to let her know she is OK. Her doubts are severe, and she continues to live at home with her folks, even though she is in her thirties.

Yvonne does not have a romantic relationship in her life, though she wants one. Although young, she is a "wise old soul," and she absorbs much energy from people she meets. She needs many clearings in our sessions, releasing the confusing energy absorbed from her family and acquaintances.

With masks and social distancing, I sensed she has even more nervous energy that needs clearing each session during this virus pandemic.

Sadly, her parents have not understood her, having her undergo too much medical treatment and medicating.

We work to assure her inner child that she is OK and she will be fine.

In our last session, I noticed that she asked for specific advice and help: she wanted clearing to attract positive people in her life and perhaps a romantic relationship. She was improving. She was less doubtful about herself than before, more focused on manifesting what she wanted, rather than doubting it, or even fearing bad outcomes.

Yvonne has made real progress toward more abundant life.

The abundance we want is waiting for us; first, we need to reduce or remove our doubts, as abundance is not just wealth, but good thoughts, good circumstances, and good people in our lives: better people, better relationships, and perhaps in Yvonne's case, even having children.

The abundance that my gift has brought into my life gives me joy and has let me share that joy with others so as to have more expansive and fulfilling lives, lives that make them and those close to them more abundantly happy.

# Chapter 4

---

# CLEARING UNCERTAINTY
# ABOUT YOUR FUTURE

**WHAT A PAIR** of years were 2020 and 2021!

The COVID-19 virus from Wuhan, China, went around the world, killing, sickening, disrupting. Political, economic, and social changes followed, and we did not know what to expect.

Will 2022 be as bad? Hard to know. We have to "hope for the best and prepare for the worst," as the adage goes.

I've seen more significant uncertainty in my life and the lives of my friends, associates, and clients. We seek some relief!

Within the last year, my personal sessions with my clients, which sessions they have purchased through telesummits, covered a broad range of topics and have often included some discussion about uncertainty, some due to the COVID virus that brought a lot of fears to my clients.

We don't know what the future holds, especially for those who have lost jobs or lost hours. These underemployed people now need to find their true gifts, looking into their hearts, reimagining, and reinvesting to get into new lines of work. This uncertainty is scary, and I help reassure them and their families.

My guidance has reflected their need to ground my clients' energy, helping them trust themselves and the universe. Further, they must learn to trust their intuition.

My sounds help them connect with their inner selves, their souls, to handle the uncertainties. I can see beyond these turbulent times, and I know life will come back to normal, somewhat different, of course, but manageable.

My gift helps my clients become grounded and be open to words of wisdom. They can hear good advice when before they might have ignored it. "Opportunity comes to the prepared mind" is credited to businessman and Berkshire Hathaway investor Charlie Munger. One needs to have one's head on straight. Our sessions bring greater day-to-day peace, and this results in clearer thinking.

"Paul" from the U.K. has had sessions with me from even before the virus. We were clearing his blocks, getting him more comfortable with his body and his work.

Lately, Paul's company has gone through a big transition due to COVID, and he lost hours, making him worry. Should he start his own business? He likes music and could do recording and selling of his vocals. His corporate job had prevented him from doing this before. His annoying boss was pushing him to look outside the company to find something better... a personality conflict that could have a good result.

Paul now realizes he need not be stuck in the job. His fears cleared in our sessions, and he started recording his music as his hours were cut.

After a few months of work, Paul's music sells online; it brings inspiration to his listeners, a sense of peace, and it induces a meditative mood. It has been selling well and may be the start of a new career.

The music is helping to pay his bills. He would not have done this unless his job situation changed and his mental condition improved. External and internal changes have produced a flourishing online business.

COVID has pushed him to a new high, a blessing, leading to his reinvention.

## Chapter 5

———— ∿ ————

# UNDERSTANDING YOUR POWERFUL POTENTIAL

DURING THIS TIME of lock-downs due to the COVID-19 virus, many clients are concerned with reinventing themselves and re-covering losses endured due to the virus. Reinvention has been an important topic.

To make a beneficial change, you need to know what you are good at and what you like, and you will do better. Some people have fallen into a groove or a pit due to the recent changes. They fear what they will face next.

Each person is unique, with a combination of strengths and weaknesses.

One client, "Sherrie," worked with me shortly before the virus hit, and we had a session that was normal for that time, a session bought through a telesummit.

That first session had been about anti-aging. Sherrie is a single mother, managing a lot of stress.

Our latest session dealt with a new job, trying to handle an unpredictable financial situation, as her ex-husband was on-again-off-again with his child support. She lives in Chicago and was making good money as a waitress at a restaurant. Her hours were cut in half, and she watched her savings evaporating.

First, we needed to determine what she was supposed to become once we cleared her fears. Her mind was racing, making it hard to think straight: fight or flight.

"Take some deep breaths and pay attention to my sounds." I made grounding sounds first. We cleared her of fear. "Is there a talent you have not been using that might make a possible new career?"

"Wow! You are right. Before kids, I was an outstanding salesperson, especially for jewelry. I made big commissions and got to wear them. I even could buy them at a discount.

"I did like making jewelry as a hobby and then selling it. When I was a waitress, people would compliment me on the pieces and even buy some."

After the session, she sent me pictures of her creations, many very pretty in a turquoise, Southwestern style.

"Why can't you sell this online?"

"So far, I only show it when I am at the restaurant."

"Why not get online with it? Some of those sites would sell it."

"I'd like to do it but am not sure I can get enough money this way for the kids and me."

"You have a fine collection here. Consider trying the Internet."

"Thanks, Dawn, you underscore what another person told me, that I should be confident enough to start selling this. I am cleared of my former fear and believe now that I can make and sell these successfully."

I had gotten her to the point where she had the confidence to try eBay and Etsy. She became excited about it.

"I'll let you know in a few months how it goes."

She called me about six weeks later, thanking me "from the bottom of her heart" because the online business was taking off, and her new clients were enthusiastic about her work.

"Wow, Dawn, I would not have done this without our session that caused me to go deeper without fear. I have both my online business and my waitressing, and I plan to expand my business and stop waitressing soon. Working for myself."

That would give her more time with her kids, another goal of hers.

In Sherrie's case and many others, when we find our true gifts, we often do these first as hobbies. Our jobs kept us from recognizing these gifts. COVID has helped some people reinvent themselves. Creating jewelry that others liked enough to buy gave her a warm feeling and gave her the confidence she lacked before. It opened her up to opportunities she had not recognized.

*Chapter 6*

# Clearing Fear of Growing Rich

**I work with** many people who have an unconscious fear, as I once feared, of receiving abundance beyond our needs.

I would just get by, week to week. I wanted more. I said affirmations in the mirror. Nothing changed. Then I had my awakening with my gift.

Awake, I learned that I was attracting scarcity, not abundance. My mother, on welfare, had set the impoverished tone for my childhood and my early adult beliefs.

"Money does not grow on trees," Mom would say. But she did not say where it did come from.

She needed to be more positive. Less negative.

I worked on myself for decades. Eventually, I healed my money wounds. I overcame my money blocks and transformed my life, coming from nothing to being prosperous and comfortable, now able to share my new knowledge with people worldwide.

Let me tell you about one of my clients, "Garett," from Switzerland.

He bought one of my abundance programs from a telesummit. He purchased a session to work on his specific issues.

"How can I help you?"

"I've always had problems with money. I get it and then lose it. I cannot hold on to it. I intend to save, but my money evaporates for this and that. A good amount of money just disappears. What can I do to stop this? I see that others can hang on to their wealth far better than I do."

"I think you do not feel worthy of your abundance. Let's do some clearing to start." We removed some of the energy effects of the COVID-19 virus pandemic, a time of fear. My sounds interacted with the energy field that was harming him.

"Take a couple of deep breaths."

I brought his life-force energy to his feet. "Better?"

"I feel calmer."

"How did your parents affect you?" His father, an alcoholic, left him and his mother after their divorce. Months would go by without seeing him, making Garrett sad. I could visualize a child waiting for his dad, hopeful, clinging to an expectation, dependent on his mother. He was now holding on to this past, stuck in a scarcity orientation. He feared loss. That negativity influenced his relationships with people as well as with money.

I described all this to him. Then I told him how we were going to address it.

"We need to clear this pattern of fear of losing everything."

He agreed.

I worked to bring to him a Divine Light to comfort his inner child; I had him imagine that child, but now being blessed by God.

"I feel that light. I am experiencing something deep now." He started crying. "I feel more healing than ever before."

We finished his session with the clearing of the residual energy problems from his childhood.

He was ecstatic. "I feel you have lifted a weight off me, and I can see the whole world as a peaceful place, and this session has given me better results than I ever had with other healers."

He thanked me profusely. He later came back for several more sessions.

Many clients come to me with deep fears of growing rich or of living comfortably above their current status. This fear derives from not being well off when younger and from not feeling deserving; sometimes they fear losing their friends if they change their status. These fears are needless. The new person will do what the old person could not.

## Chapter 7

<hr />

# CLEARING FEAR OF MOVING FORWARD

IN THIS TIME of uncertainty due to the COVID virus, many of my clients have experienced changes that worry them about the future, especially about the financial future. They have endured financial hardship due to downsizing, cutting of hours, loss of clients.

Recent sessions with clients have often centered on making plans for successful futures, clearing their fears, aligning the clients more with their souls, and getting them more energy.

One client's wife, Ann, bought a session for herself and then another for her husband, William.

William and I worked together, and he had never worked with an energy -healer before. COVID had changed so much in their lives that he and Ann were willing to look for answers in unconventional places. His unemployment payments had recently run out. He felt up against the wall, economically. What could he do to help support his family?

He permitted me to work with his energy, especially removing his fears and generating ideas for a new way to obtain income.

I first cleared his energy of the fear he had absorbed from people around him. We cleared his aura, his energy field. We focused next on job prospects.

We worked on his breathing while I made my clearing sounds.

"How are you feeling?"

"I feel something has moved within me. I'm feeling lighter and less anxious; my wife has worked with you, and I have seen her change a lot, positively, which is why I decided to try working with you."

I saw we were successful in redirecting his energy. He had many fears brought up by this treatment, and we cleared them.

Much of his fear came from the childhood experience of having an unusually fearful father, eventually leaving William chronically constipated. We worked on relieving this feeling. His stomach responded with gurgling sounds.

"I can see you have done many different jobs in your past. You are a bit confused about what to do now that you lost this most recent position."

"Yes, I am."

"I can tell," I said, "you are a people-person, open and gregarious, and you need to look in that direction."

He replied, "But the virus makes that harder, harder to meet safely and comfortably with people."

He used to be a part-time Uber driver, which he enjoyed but had to stop with the reduction of that business due to people fearing the virus.

I tried to reassure him, "Everybody is wearing masks now, and perhaps you could continue to do that kind of work safely."

"Maybe so. I'll look into it again. I'd also like to work helping people with their problems, as a counselor. When I did that as a driver, they even ended up giving me bigger tips!"

William decided to retry Uber and do some eBay merchandising. He could do both safely. The session had helped him bring forward several alternatives he had not seen at its start due to his fears.

"I'm going to get back to doing some Uber and eBay, and I thank you for helping me get unstuck."

Yes, that is something I like to do with my clients, help them generate useful ideas for themselves. With an unusual situation like that due to COVID, we need to adopt some new approaches or revive things we had once discarded.

# Chapter 8

---

# Seeing Your Future Clearly

**The COVID virus** has had me helping people to see what comes next, having had their lives disrupted so thoroughly.

Significant life changes have happened. Many people have lost their confidence that the future will be better rather than worse.

My job as a healer goes beyond mind and body to their Soul and their trust in their inner guidance. They need something they can trust.

One client, "Kate," is a single mom with three sons, all in grammar school. Before COVID, she lived on one of the Hawaiian Islands, and we had worked together to handle her divorce and some romantic and commercial activities.

Kate's husband was a dead-beat dad, but she could handle it, pre-COVID. She managed cleaning condos, and there were lots of tourists who needed that. She would sell flower leis, delivering them to restaurants.

All of that changed in 2020 due to the virus.

We had a session a few months into the pandemic. Both businesses had tanked, had come to a halt, the quarantine was so strict.

What should she do? How could a flower business stop? No tourists, restaurants were going bankrupt.

Her businesses had been her future, and now they were failing. No traffic.

"What do I do to support myself and my three sons?"

We started our session with my clearing her energy, as it was filled with turmoil and fear and negative emotion. We grounded her energy for about ten minutes. Later, we not only stabilized her energy, but I also connected with her Soul to help her fear the future less.

Although a fine businesswoman, she needed reassurance and some ideas about alternative paths and attitudes. She was connected with a flower farm, where the leis were made. I suggested she sell the leis online, rather than just at the restaurants.

"That's a good idea. I had not thought of that. I could use a website or put them on eBay. You make me think I can do it."

"Yes, your new endeavor will help you, and you will help the farmer who has the flowers. You can ship directly to the Islands and the Mainland."

"I know someone with a dry ice facility that could enable me to send these overseas. I had not thought of that until we spoke today. Great idea!"

She got excited. Somehow, our session was what she needed to get a clearer view of a promising future.

"I have a website I have ignored, but now I am excited about getting it going again." She looked relieved.

"How do you feel now, Kate?"

"Much more inspired. I feel I am back on track."

A few months later, she got another session with me.

"Kate, how are you doing?"

"I got on it right away, and it channeled my energy. It magically came together as the farmer and a packaging professional connected with us. I wouldn't have had the insight or courage to do this without your inspiration. I know it will grow, as these flowers are getting wonderful responses. Word of mouth is getting me business, and those who cannot visit here get a charge out of having some of our beautiful flowers."

We did some more grounding during the session, and she reported she was more inspired, looking forward to redoing her condo-cleaning and restaurant-supply activities once tourism resumes.

"We are going to be OK," Kate affirmed.

I am finding that some of my clients are making changes after reassessing themselves and their situations, even during this difficult time. They are open to my non-traditional approach, forced by the circumstances to try something new, and they are getting value from doing so. They see a new future much more clearly and with heightened enthusiasm.

## Chapter 9

# CLEARING DISORGANIZATION

WHEN I WAS homeless during my spiritual journey, my life was very disorganized, especially physically, as I lived out of a car for six months without knowing when or where I would get my next meal. I had hocked my jewelry in a local pawn shop. I lived mainly on McDonald's Dollar Meals for those six months!

I had rented a Rent-a-Wreck car with the little money I brought with me. I had once been wealthy, but my two dysfunctional marriages had left me broke.

"Follow my heart" became my mantra. I started to pick up little jobs, getting enough money to have a deposit on a rental apartment, one with clean running water and a bed and safety. That achieved getting more organized!

My healing gift came to me toward the end of this period. Two decades later, I have become a well-known and well-organized speaker, writer, and life-changer.

I am now the most organized I have ever been! One trick: the simple, necessary things in life come first.

One of my clients, "Belinda," was my first landlord. My gift was being developed then, and she recognized this. She was good to me. I lived there for ten years. However, the home/business property was a chaotic mess. They loved animals so much, they let them get out of hand! Dogs, cats, parrots, turtles...it was wild.

That chaos, which Belinda was accustomed to, was not working well for me. The rent was cheap, however, and Belinda was sweet, but her family hoarded. Nothing was discarded. Craziness. Living there was disorganizing.

"Belinda, is having all this stuff working well for you?"

"I appreciate your asking me about that. I fear discarding anything, Dawn, because I might need it in the future."

"Let me help you with some of the counter-productive beliefs that are harming you. The birdcages in the backyard are mixed in with furniture, etc., and customers are puzzled. The set-up is not good *feng shui*, the Chinese would say. You have been so good to me, and I want to help you. Sit here. Listen to my sounds; they will clear your mind chatter."

I made my sounds. I also told her, "Breathe more deeply, and release that pent-up energy."

I detected much sadness located in her stomach. Her elderly father lived with her but was emotionally distant from her, and she tried to please him without success.

"Belinda, let's clear some more stress." I relieved the stress in her stomach, bringing the excess energy to her feet and into the ground, thus "grounding" her.

"How do you feel now?'"

"Great!"

"Yes, some of your beliefs were contributing to your disorganization, but I have cleared these for you."

A week went by, but nothing seemed to have changed with all the clutter. Had the session not been productive?

I was relieved when Belinda told me, "I've contacted the Salvation Army, and they will come with a big truck, and we will be donating the stuff to help people who are homeless and jobless. I no longer care about all these objects. I feel much better now.

"The birds even seem more tranquil, and the customers seem to like it better, and we are getting more people coming here and photographing the birds. Somehow you shifted my life, making me more positive, inspired, and peaceful. I don't know how you did it, but you have brought me more abundance, and I greatly appreciate it. Thank you for all your help."

In the case of Belinda, and for me for that time, our environment was so disorganized that it disorganized us, and my treatments for her helped her get mentally free and declutter her life. This practice helped to clear the negative emotions and the disorganization that makes everything harder to accomplish.

With more organization, things come more easily, almost without asking. You might call this new orderliness "spiritual *feng shui*," from which we derive more peace and abundance.

## Chapter 10

# CLEARING INHERITED BELIEFS

**MANY CLIENTS I** have worked with have come to me with trouble moving toward their abundance goals over the years.

Their energies are often blocked.

Why do they have trouble? When I do their sessions, we go back to their childhoods and learn about possible traumas, including abuse.

Surprisingly, I find in some cases no childhood traumas. So that's not it.

From where do their problems come? Going deeper, I find ancestral, inherited energetic issues. The problems arise from there.

Having pinpointed these energy distortions, these blockages, I then can free up their energy. They are unbound, and the distortions in their energy fields are repaired.

Recently, I worked with a man from the U.K., a continuing client, "John," who has bought many of my telesummit sessions to get to my personal sessions.

For John, we have cleared many areas of his life. He is an "old soul," one who has had many reincarnations. We work on distortions from the past that are affecting him now.

He has had romances, has had significant others, fathered no children.

He loves his profession, in computers, at a respected U.K. company. His progress there is blocked, leaving him stressed out. His boss is negative, requiring John to handle a discouraging situation.

We have worked together several times.

In this Covid-19 pandemic year of 2020, he felt stuck.

"What could I do to change this? I want a new direction."

We had our sound session. Afterwards, I asked, "What is happening, John?"

"I still feel stuck."

Even so, he goes to work every day, feeling stressed by his coworkers.

A thorough energy clearing helped. We entered into the light.

Ancestral energy blocks became evident. They have caused him confusion. On his father's side, two generations back, the family had a financial business that went broke. His grandfather and the family suffered.

"Wow! Even my grandfather in his lifetime had severe lack-consciousness."

I replied, "He was doing his best, carrying the family weight, as you are now. You are clearing your ancestral energy, and this will help your children in the future to a brighter future."

We went through a clearing process for his whole family, using my sounds.

"Wow! I actually feel energy releasing."

After another six minutes of my sounds, "Wow! I am feeling the energy moving. I'm no longer clogged."

"Take some deep breaths, as you have done a lot of work today. In the coming month, see how your life changes."

At the start of our next session, I checked with John.

"How are you doing after last month's session?"

"Full of life. Feeling lighter. The session was a life-changer. I felt the energy surge for three days, followed by the feeling of having a protective blanket. I saw with a new light. It is exciting. Shining energy. I am resuming playing the guitar and doing other things I love. I can get into the studio and record an album once the virus passes. Clearing that inherited condition, I now look forward to getting up each day, with a spring in my step, a miracle. Thank you so very much. I'm inspired.

## Chapter 11

~~~

# BECOME YOUR BEST SELF

PART OF MY work with my clients, besides clearing their unconscious blocks, is telling them some things they need to know: what is their truth, their Soul's calling, why they are here on Earth, what their best self is like.

I find that our minds can help us know what we are supposed to do, to awaken spiritually, to know what it is we should be doing. Not to erase what we know about ourselves, but to put us in contact with our true selves, deepening what we are doing.

This is mindfulness of our self-purpose, and it will affect our work, our family, our community, and ourselves and our eternal joy.

With your mind clear, you become more intuitive, knowing what you want rather than what you mistakenly think you want.

Deeper in our hearts lies the answers to what we should be doing. We have to open ourselves, like a blossoming flower, to become our true selves.

I have worked with "Emily" several times; she is an old soul living in a young body. She's had a rocky life. We met through telesummits. Our sessions have changed over time. I have to go with what she is available to receive. She is surrounded by people who do not understand her, who see her as weird. She is an outcast.

After I worked with Emily several times, as she has bought several of my sessions, we have focused on finding her true purpose. She needed clearing of the static in her mind and body that she picked up from others, as she is empathic, a sensitive soul.

We cleared many anxieties, which threatened to overtake her. Her other healers have not been successful, despite their use of unconventional techniques. Her parents were from Eastern Europe, in the Soviet Union, and they experienced much fear in that environment. They were working-class people. She got to America at age two, eventually granted citizenship here.

Despite the advantages of being in America, she was a sensitive soul in a strange land, and her parents struggled economically, given that their language skills were limited. Emily shouldered her parents' woes, trying to make their lives better, almost parenting them rather than having them parent her. Their family life was chaotic.

In our sessions, deeper and deeper we went. Emily began escaping survival mode into a mode where she could release the old trauma of her parents' lives and begin to enjoy her life. Fear was being driven out, replaced by hope.

ABUNDANCE MADE CRYSTAL CLEAR!

That is not unlike other clients I have had, as fear energy is transmitted from one generation to another. A conscious person must stop this chain reaction. I was working not only on Emily, but also on her family, in effect.

Toward the end of one session, I said, "Take a deep breath. How are you feeling now?"

"Much better. I feel I have new lenses in my eyes, and a heavy weight has been taken off my shoulders."

"You have been carrying your whole family's worries and fears and depression."

She has since then started to think about what she wants to do, what will bring her joy and abundance.

Amazingly, at the end of that session, she started to laugh and giggle, and she told me this was the first ime in years she had done that.

We ended with a grounding session, connecting her with her soul, continuing to expel the negative energies derived from her family.

A month later, in a beautiful session, we did not deal with trauma, but directed our thoughts to her gaining a life partner.

She is going to contact me to tell me how she is doing.

For Emily and many of my clients with whom I have worked over the years, the early sessions have to do with urgent issues, such as dealing with family trauma. Later sessions move from clearing pain to moving toward joy and abundance. In these sessions, they connect with their soul's purpose.

In my own life, aligning with my purpose has brought me abundance and happiness, finding opportunities and skills I never knew I could have. Thus began my life's work.

*Chapter 12*

CLEARING BLOCKS INTO
RECEIVING MORE

IN MY EARLIER life, I lived many years from hand to mouth, with just enough to get by, nothing left over. I envied those who had a lot, but I never knew how to get more than what I needed. Some people brought in scads of money every year, and I just scraped along.

My negative beliefs were that these people had gotten the breaks that I did not get. I wasted time being jealous, making myself miserable. I wanted those luxury items that I could not afford, and I lacked the wisdom to understand why.

My awakening in my mid-thirties changed all that. I started to clear myself of my trauma. Then, I got clear on what was happening, why I was just getting by.

I was attracting what I was born into, what I spent my time thinking about, what the people around me thought was enough. I had to clear the trauma, then clear the blocks to receiving more than just necessities. It took me years. Things changed, and my outlook on life changed with them.

I now work with clients who recognize me world-wide as a person who helps them receive more, well beyond just their needs, helping them live lives they truly desire and deserve.

Many of my clients seek abundance-block-clearing in our sessions. They want my help to remove the blocks to their receiving more.

"Philip" is a gentleman from the UK who is already a successful importer/exporter. He purchased one of my telesummit programs.

This first time I worked with him, I asked him what he would like help with.

"I make a lot of money in import-export, but somehow it slips through my hands, just disappears."

"How long has this been going on?"

"My whole life. I have a good business mind, know how to make money, but not how to keep it."

"May I look into your energy?"

"Yes. I'd be grateful."

During this successful session, we investigated his ancestral energy sources. He was carrying the energy from past generations of relatives who did not even have enough food for the winter months. His parents had this same feast-or-famine energy.

I asked him if he realized this was coming from a very deep level, one he probably was not aware of. He began to understand. I told him, "This is coming to you from your ancestors. Are you ready to clear this energy?"

"Yes," he said, "definitely!"

"I will release this energy that should not be yours." I made my sounds to remove his feast-or-famine toxic energy. He started to cry. I reassured him, "This energy is not properly yours; it is from your ancestors."

He became light-headed, and I made sounds to ground him to Planet Earth. When I was done, I had him breathe deeply, and I asked him how he felt.

"Wow! I feel so much lighter. A heavy weight has been taken off my shoulders."

We ended the session. I advised him to drink more water than usual for a few days, as part of the transformation process.

He was to contact me in a few weeks. He did so, by email, and he told me that he could see a difference in his company's performance, his own income, and his ability to keep from wasting his money. He intends to return for another session.

I am always pleased to help my clients remove the blocks that keep them from harnessing the universal flow of true abundance.

*Chapter 13*

CLEARING INTERNAL BLOCKS

SOMETIMES, WE SABOTAGE ourselves with internal blocks.

"Behavior is said to be self-sabotaging when it creates problems in daily life and interferes with long-standing goals. The most common self-sabotaging behaviors include procrastination, self-medication with drugs or alcohol, comfort eating, and forms of self-injury such as cutting.

"People aren't always aware that they are sabotaging themselves, and connecting a behavior to self-defeating consequences is no guarantee that a person will disengage from it. Still, it is possible to overcome almost any form of self-sabotage. Behavioral therapies can aid in interrupting ingrained patterns of thought and action while strengthening deliberation and self-regulation. Motivational therapies can also help reconnect people with their goals and values." [*Psychology Today*|Self-sabotage]

Growing up, I lived with chaos: my mother had six kids in our dysfunctional, welfare family. No praise. Lots of insecurities. There was no money to get things or do things like participating in my dreamed-of grammar school dancing lessons.

I was almost always on my own, often forced to the sidelines. Yet, I kept moving forward, with an internal will that told me there had to be more in life.

By sixteen, I was plowing through life, working against my self-sabotage. I was going to "get to the other side."

I became a police officer a few years after I graduated from high school. This was a success. I married, then nursed my fellow-officer husband for years before we divorced.

After marriage, I had opened my own businesses, overcoming self-sabotage that made it hard for me to move forward.

No one congratulated me. I was still on my own, as I am now.

Let me describe the work I did with a recent client.

"Bertha" lives in Italy. She worked with me through several Skype sessions. Despite being highly educated, she had a self-sabotage problem: her husband, an alcoholic, lived off her, riding on her coattails. Before this marriage, she had been very successful.

"I've been married to him for ten years, and I love him very much, but he has been negative and dependent."

She had been a successful clothing designer. However, the marriage sapped her energy. She started to believe herself to be unable to compete well against other talented designers.

"What else do you believe?"

"I think my competitors in clothing design can design less expensive lines."

I got to know her story.

"Bertha, your negative husband and his disrespect can have bad impacts. His threats to take all you own, though a divorce, understandably worry you."

With me, Bertha has been clearing some of these blockages, and she has gotten the courage to leave her husband.

During one session, we worked on the beliefs from her childhood that arose when her father left her mother. Her mother struggled after that, with three kids and little income.

Her life in some ways repeated what her mother had endured.

I told her, "We have to clear this mental story. These beliefs are not reality. We can clear these fears forced on you. You can come into the light once you let these go.

"Now, we shift to the present moment."

We cleared her fears about her business. She came to realize she creates her own life, with her gifts that attract others to her. She came to understand that she did not have to stay with her husband. She saw that her husband could not conquer her. Her power could prevail.

I reconnected her to the Earth, draining negative energy and gaining positive energy. Her personal power grew as she released her fears.

"How do you feel now, after our work?"

"No longer worried. If you could see me, you'd see I have a beautiful smile on my face, and my heart feels expanded."

"Are you worried about leaving your husband?"

"I don't care. I can leave him. He is not the right person for me."

She planned to contact me after seeing how these changes affected her life.

Later, I did get an email from her. She thanked me profusely. She has filed for divorce and has opened a new contract with a firm in the UK that will support her line of designer clothes. She wrote that her self-sabotaging thoughts had previously not allowed her to "step out of the box" in business and marriage.

As I have explained, I have cleared self-sabotaging beliefs that hold us back from true joy and abundance in my life and with my clients. Over many years, I have been happy to have changed many people's lives, fulfilling their lives as I fulfill mine.

# Chapter 14

∽

# CLEARING FEELING WORTHLESS

FOR MOST OF my early life, I felt worthless. My self-esteem was zero.

My single-parent mother was absorbed in making ends meet, not in making us feel loved. An older brother was addicted to drugs and alcohol, and all I witnessed was people putting themselves down and putting me down—no positive reinforcement. School was hell, and my learning disabilities put me at a real disadvantage, yet I made it through high school and even some college.

What was I doing? What was my future? A puzzle!

Still, I always had the feeling that I had something in my heart keeping me on track, and that feeling persisted even as I became an adult. Call it "an inner compass" or "my soul," I finally connected with it when I went homeless, after my second marriage, when I experienced a spiritual awakening.

Trial and error got me some successes, especially in my police career (top woman athlete in my class, with many awards, including a special recommendation to serve in any Chicago district.)

After my second marriage, my beauty businesses started from the ground up also began to thrive, despite my lack of business training and experience. My inner guide helped. The companies were successful for as long as I had them, but a toxic marriage caused me to abandon them.

After my second divorce, I felt worthless and sad. Somewhat later, as a homeless person, I found a source of feeling worthwhile when I discovered my gift at helping people heal, a power I used on myself first before sharing it with others.

Having healed myself made me feel worthy. I decided all my experiences had brought me to a special place. Now I share my gift worldwide with those ready to connect abundantly with their inner compasses, their souls.

Yesterday, I had a session with Diane, who had worked with me a year before. Now she needed clearing of past feelings of worthlessness. Her growing up had been in a family situation similar to my own.

Last year, Diane and I had worked on clearing her pre-birth energy. She, too, is an "old soul," more aware than most people.

"What do you want to work on today?"

"I feel my life is worthless. I work in a job as a nanny, a job I like, one with nice people. A romantic relationship a few years ago was disempowering. At 54, I need to know how to have more life, as mine feels empty. I'd like to have love in my life."

We had cleared some pre-birth energies last year, from her conception to birth. This time we worked on childhood traumas from around the ages of 4 and 5, where she watched her father beat her mother.

"That is terrible. You picked up much of your mother's pain. You absorbed your mother's helplessness. You tried to share her pain to make your mother's load lighter. Breathe deeply. Are you ready to release these negative memories and energy?"

"Yes, this is depressing me."

I cleared her heart and stomach of these energies that she had been bearing her whole life. They had made Diane feel unworthy of anything good that came to her.

Her past was ruining her present.

She started to cry as I was moving her energy.

I worked on her for several minutes, and after that, I had her take a deep breath.

"How are you feeling?"

Her crying stopped. She started laughing and giggling!

"Wow! I don't know where this came from, but I think this is energy that I have kept suppressed, holding it for others. I feel lighter and much happier. Happiest I have ever felt!"

She kept laughing uncontrollably, peals of joy.

Later, I had her take another deep breath.

"How do you feel?"

"Oh, my God, I feel so alive right now. I cannot thank you enough for your gift. I feel on top of the world, and I can conquer anything."

"Do you feel worthy?"

"Yes, worthy of this happiness."

We ended our call.

So, over twenty years, I have seen my gift help others, as though I am connecting with their souls. I cleared the next level for Diane, after the level we had worked on a year before. I created a whole new way of life for her. She has a new way to live a life that she never believed was possible.

I have had this experience with clients finding their true essences to give them back joy and abundance.

## *Chapter 15*

## CLEARING YOUR DEBTS

MY LIFE AS a child included having a first job at nine, a paper route, to get clothing for school.

At 16, I had a few jobs, one as a restaurant hostess, and another in a donut shop. I lacked guidance, so I tended to accept credit card offers sent to me in the mail. Being naïve, I piled up a lot of credit card debt. I had about a half-dozen cards. Nevertheless, I enjoyed myself getting things I always wanted. I got through the special offers, and the bills started coming.

"OMG! I've got to pay for all this." Over the next few years, I was just paying off the interest on the cards. My folks could not help. I was covering my school costs, including walking there rather than taking a car or public trasnortation.

I finally paid off my credit card debt, working as a marketer for a large plastics corporation. I took a decade to clear what I spent plus the interest. A valuable lesson! Such cards are addictive; you had to avoid them.

I returned to my free-spending ways later, and I filed for bankruptcy. I learned that these cards are not my friends. If I cannot pay cash, it is not for me. "Cash and carry or do not tarry." That was my hard lesson regarding debt.

A realistic adage goes, "It's an ill wind that blows nobody any good." Some storms take you to new places where you prosper. So it has been with the Covid-19 pandemic.

Some clients have money problems caused by the Covid catastrophe. They had favorable pre-Covid earning and spending patterns upended by the illness.

Lily, a mother of four living in Florida, a successful interior designer, lost her business during Covid. We had several sessions then.

She was beside herself as she watched her business spiral down.

"How will I pay for my store, support my employees, keep my home?' She needed help.

In our first session, we had to clear her paralyzing fear. Calming her helped her, and as we did it, some answers came, some soul guidance. Next, she had to change what she was doing. She burdened herself with too much overhead. She had to negotiate with her landlord to get a pause or reduction in rent. She did arrange to get a half-year pause.

In our second session, she got a message from her soul that she should also negotiate with her mortgage company, which she soon did successfully, a big help. Furthermore, her credit card debt needed attention. With little income, she was able to get a compromise with her credit card companies. One gave her a consolidation loan, saving her much monthly money through an affordable home equity loan. The situation became manageable.

In session three, we addressed: how about her lost income? She had four children. All had developed and enjoyed the habit of eating. She once had been active in creative endeavors, such as making decorative wallpaper or artistic jewelry. She could return to doing some of that, this session revealed. She could sell some that she had made earlier. She agreed. She decided to revive her own counseling business, even using some of the insights gained from our sessions, which pleased me.

In our session four, still during Covid, we again checked her energy, and it was clear she was a lot calmer.

In session five, she reported getting more business. Her counseling endeavor was taking off! She began making more money than before, even more than with the interior design projects, and now she was doing work she preferred. She has reinvented herself!

The "ill winds" of Covid provided elements of creative destruction, proving to my clients they have abilities, once dormant, that could help them and others find new success. Some of the re-awakenings brought my clients to new paths they enjoyed more than where they trod pre-covid.

The pandemic sometimes proved a blessing in disguise.

## Chapter 16

# CLEARING LACK-CONSCIOUSNESS

**LACK-CONSCIOUSNESS FOR ME** started with my parents. As early as I can remember, growing up, all I used to hear was, "We do not have enough."

Anything I wanted as a child, big or small, I could not get. My welfare mom was the product of parents of the Depression. She grew up this way. Her parents had very little.

This phrase became ingrained in my mind: "We do not have enough."

Especially when I was in my earlier years of working, during my school years, starting at age nine with that paper route, I wanted to support myself because my mom believed we had not enough to give me anything extra.

Most of my early life was lived hand-to-mouth. Money would leave me as soon as I got it.

Even as an adult, I could not hold on to money, either, It would come, and it would go, sometimes being gone before I even got it.

I never saved a dime.

Later, I realized the truth, during my spiritual awakening: I had to work on my belief system, as I have been doing ever since then. I am overcoming my lack-consciousness.

The wisdom I gained, I share with my clients. My telesummit programs I offer at a reasonable price. But what I offer has price-less value.

Recently, Joanne from the U.K. bought one of my programs, one about abundance. On the phone, I could tell she was nervous, unsure. I'd guess she is about 70; she is married, with a husband not open to such spiritual work.

"How can I help you?" I asked Joanne.

"I want to receive more in my life, more abundance. We have been living on a very basic level. Just getting by. Barely enough to pay the bills, No extra money for vacations and the like."

"Tell me about your childhood. How did your parents treat you?"

"I came from an Eastern European country, formerly part of the USSR, a poor environment."

"Were your parents loving and giving to you?"

"They fled that country, and we came to England. We were poor, struggling refugees. My folks worked long hours, making very little money. Food and a roof, that was about it."

"Did your parents complain about money during your childhood?"

"Yes, all the time. How would we pay the rent? How buy food? I left home and married just to escape to get a better life."

She and her husband have been married for over 50 years. Concerning money worries, he is something like her parents, not as much so, She feels "blessed" with two adult children and two grandchildren, and she would like to give that youngest generation a better life. Her dream is to take the grandchildren to the U.S. to Disney World. The kids have pictures of Disney characters all over their bedrooms.

"I want to work on receiving more abundance to share with these children."

"Take a deep breath, and we are going to start clearing out the blocks."

I did a clearing of lack-consciousness, using my sounds and having her envision a bright light over her head.

I could detect that deep down, she was afraid to have money.

"Joanne, would you like to clear your fear of having money?"

"Absolutely!"

We cleared this belief system right out of her heart! That negative energy left her heart, going up into the light above her head.

"Take another deep breath. How are you feeling now? You have been cleared of your belief in the reality of lack."

She started laughing, "Wow, I actually have a smile on my face from ear to ear. I have a sense of relief on a deep level that I have never felt before." She said her eyes seemed to see more clearly. "I am feeling a sense of peace and happiness that I have never felt."

"Pay attention to what you want, every day, not to what you don't want. Your thinking will bring to you the situation you desire."

We then proceeded to clear her life-force energy. She said she had never felt this good, and she was going to email me and tell me how things were going.

Two weeks after her session, she did email me; she told me that one of her husband's distant family members left money for them in a will they had known nothing about. An attorney had contacted them a week after our session and told them there was a substantial amount of money in their names; this turned out to be a dream come true.

Once the inheritance money is in their bank account, she will be getting tickets to Disney World for herself and her grandchildren!

Joanne thanked me warmly, sincerely. She thanked me for the gift of clarity from our session, far beyond what she expected, "a magical, life-changing experience."

It is common for my clients and me to have come from childhoods where we wrongly learned that life is lack, and this lack-consciousness affects our entire life. The main thing is for us to tell our children that life is abundance, not scarcity, and for us to be careful what we say in their presence. Emphasize plenty, not poverty.

We can be more, and we can have more than we think we can.

# Chapter 17

———❧———

# OPENING UP TO THE UNIVERSAL FLOW OF ABUNDANCE

As a result of all the 20 years I have been doing the work of clearing out my belief system from the baggage of my childhood, using the healing techniques that I share with my clients, I have learned we all are connected; we are all creatures on this planet. There is a generous Creator. Nature is so abundant. We must be blocking that abundance if we are suffering from scarcity. To fix that, we need to feel worthy of receiving, especially of receiving love and plenty.

I have opened my life to the universal flow of abundance, which comes to me from the Divine. I connect with beneficial people, ideas, and opportunities as a result.

My goal with some of my clients is to connect them to their flow of abundance. They need blockages removed, allowing them to know they are deserving of well-being. Sometimes it takes only one session together, but other times we have to work through several until we reach the "Wow!" moment, where new insight changes them dramatically.

"Yasmin" I have worked with several times, a woman from Eastern Europe who follows me on the telesummits and has purchased numerous sessions with me. She responds enthusiastically to my sound sessions that she finds help her relax and "think straight."

Our sessions revolve around removing "brain static" that confuses her. She has a lot of fear that keeps her from thinking as well as she might. Perhaps this is because her ancestors were victims of oppression in their culture.

She has recently wanted us to focus on increasing her energy toward achieving her goals for prosperity. She has taken on much responsibility for others, which is generous, and she has a good heart, trying to make others feel better, but she has been absorbing their negative energy, causing her static.

Yasmin is aware of the universal flow of goodness and knows she needs to discard the barriers that are keeping her from it.

Yasmin's brain has been wired to make her want to help others, partly because she has felt unworthy. As we cleared this energy, I believed it would be solving the problem of her feeling undeserving.

"Yasmin, we are working well today, clearing lots of negative energy."

She replied, "Wow! I feel like I am expanding with warm, positive energy." She took a few deep breaths, "I feel we have broken through to a new level. I am more motivated and feel more deserving of success. My mind is clearer than in the past few years. I feel happier."

After the session, she emailed me that she has received the opportunity to get a job that would pay her three times what she was making! She also met someone toward whom she was romantically inclined. I could hear the excitement in Yasmin's voice. We will work together to continue to access this flow of deserved good fortune.

# Chapter 18

## SUMMING UP

**WORKING ON MYSELF** almost from birth to this day has been a learning curve for me, giving me lessons to share with others.

It seems everything in my life has taught me something worth knowing.

Abundance for me was a challenge, having grown up with almost nothing. I had to create my own abundance, lacking a teacher. Now I can teach others what I learned.

What did I really want? Not to destroy my life the way my family had destroyed theirs. I knew it was to be sink or swim for my life, and I decided to swim.

I came to achieve what I had not thought possible. As a child, I dreamed about a magical life.

As an adult, I worked on self-improvement, surrounding myself with successful and positive people.

My successes at work reassured me I could do even more. Those childhood voices that said I could not succeed were pushed out of my mind by a clearer picture of my life, telling me why the struggle had been necessary. Challenge brought growth.

By working with my clients worldwide for more than 20 years, my skills sharpened, leaving me grateful for having the knowledge to share with any client from any culture, connecting on a deep soul level. These meetings allow me to help align their physical beings and their souls to obtain their highest well-being. Their bodies and spirits need to be joined, making them more alive, more joyful, attracting abundance – more than money – plugged into life on all levels.

My high success rate with clients, demonstrated by their testimonials and many requests for return meetings, helps me align each soul with its original, divine blueprint, bringing mental and physical abundance beyond limits.

We can always learn from others. My stories help my clients not repeat the mistakes I have made or mistakes other clients have made.

Such holistic techniques can remove the obstacles to achieving our deepest desires.

If you want my help, I offer many different tools on my website, where much free material is provided: http://www.dawncrystal-healing.com. The site also includes information on my programs and personal sessions.

# TESTIMONIALS

These testimonials have been received by Dawn from those she has helped. We have made only minor revisions, primarily for readability and privacy.

Hello Dawn, I just had the tremendous blessing of listening to your session through Eram Saeed's weight loss seminar. Your master class was wonderful and very intriguing. Thank you for the wonderful information and providing a different approach to healing. May God richly bless you.

Kind Regards,

C

I have hearing aids and this you tube channel of Dawn helping others cleared my ears; she's getting louder and louder.* I have two implants by the way. it'll be maybe 4 months before I get my new teeth. * that will be another process to the finish <3

J

Thank you, once again for tonight's session!

Amazingly warm, personalized, devoted and care-full!

Already feel more in peace and energized!

Thank you for the advises!

The whole experience exceeded my expectations!

Wishing you always all the best!

Love, Light and Blessings,

V

Hello,

I want to THANK YOU for the "work" that you do... I loved my one on one with you and the two programs that I purchased are uplifting - always feel lighter, taller, open, and freer when I listen... Peace and love your way...

K

Dawn

Thank you for helping me release pains when you were on webinar on Tue, October 29th. I was miserable, not feeling well with having some physical conditions, and I was in bed when I was joining the webinar.

I am feeling much better and did restart a small exercise on the next day even 30 min walk, and I realized whose work is very helpful to me. I could not do exercise about almost one year until I got help from you.

I am responsible for my life, and I don't intend to create dependency with or to anyone. But it is OK for everyone to get help as necessary. Dawn is the one I would ask for help or buy product when I need to boost my energy.

Only products from others working for me are entity clearing and ancestral karmas.

I didn't do energy work on my own, but also did start belief clearing again after few weeks break.

I appreciate if you have a class like learning strategy course you regularly offer biweekly for 6 months. I can afford to join the course or do wait for any discount sales sometimes you inform via your email newsletter.

Two products I bought from purelight especially stomach one ...I keep playing it when I can play without tech destruction.

I wanted to express sincere gratitude to you, Dawn, who helped me tremendously and the results what I got from this week's webinar was just beyond words.

N

Dawn,

Your generosity of Spirit and Compassion touches and humbles and inspires me each time we we've worked together. Thank you.

(And I'm still heartburn free, Woo-HOO! ).

Love,

P

Hi Dawn,

What a Joy! I no longer need to cringe or contract when some traumatic experience raises up within me! Now I Feel it and Release it into God's Light, Poof! Gone!

You had asked where I had bought our 10/30/19 session from. I believe it was from the Eram Saeed, From Heartache to Joy, show and the package was Organ Regeneration.

It was like I heard your voice in my head, "order Whatever you want to eat for dinner!". So, I did, I had Italian, and, there was absolutely No heartburn afterwards! YAY! Thank you!!

Love, P

Hello Dawn,

I had to write to thank you for our phone time together (part of Eram's package offer) on Oct 7th.

Where you led us in that conversation was truly insightful; to a place haven't been able to go and examine with anyone before (including myself!). It had to do with extreme vaginal dryness for years and your insight to a mother/son relationship for 37 years of marriage to a man I dearly love! husband being a son in another lifetime. I struggled with that for over a week but allowed the reality and healing and shift to happen.

After several days I felt a very large physical vaginal opening to receive him (although still sore and dry). He picked up on something as well and he started to talk more about this. So that healing opened that other door to communicate better about our sexual life, and how frustrated he has been feeling for years that I may to want to receive him. Wow!

And chronic head pressure!! For years! It has lessened and I've improved so much! Nowhere near as intense. I'm thrilled that your love, care, and sound truly lifted that pressure!

I know you receive a lot of letters so you may or may not get to read this which is OK ...LOL I just had to write you! You are truly a gifted healer, and I send my love, gratitude and deep appreciation to you, dearest Dawn.

Love, F

Hola Dawn,

It's been 2 yrs since my last healing session with you. You helped me and my dog Cleo, who was diagnosed with cancer in the liver. She transitioned on 1-11-2018/11 and my time with her was special after our session with you.

I am writing in regard to another special friend her name is Kita. She's 16.5yrs and will be transitioning soon. She is resilient. strong and full of life. She's not ready to let go yet and I feel she may have some messages for me and the family.

We would love a 30min session for her to receive messages and some energy clearing for her to make her transition that much easier and full of love.

Please advise as to which package you have for pets.

Gracias, Dawn, looking forward to reconnecting with you.

D

Hi Liz,

I'm writing to thank you and Dawn for the session I had last Monday at 7pm (BST). I am so grateful to Dawn for all she did for me. I am with her Learning Strategies group since the second series. She worked so hard for me and gave me such strength. I am so sorry for the hassle with skype and so grateful to you Liz for letting me call your cell phone. I honestly can't tell you both how much the session strengthened me. And it continues to do so. I am so looking forward to Sound Healing Series #5!

Thank you both so much. Wishing you both a lovely day!

O.

Ireland

Hi Dawn,

I hope this finds all is well with you and your Pupp.

Just a quick update....

For the First Time since the back injury occurred over 4 years ago, I can turn completely around to my right side! I really Appreciate that you sent the Complete, "Get Out of Pain Forever" Package. Your Compassionate Response is so very much Appreciated. I'd felt waves of relief move over me as I listened to the "Clearing Back Pain" module. The pain has improved Tremendously.

And, Thanks So Much for sending along the Wealth Revolution "Personal Awakening" package. I have felt unwinding and releases as I've listened to the Beautiful Music.

I continue to shake my head in Wonder and Joy at the Blessings from all the different modules.

From my Heart to Yours, Thank You Dawn!

Dawn

I recently bought the "Getting out of pain" pkg from Soul Talk, I'm wondering if the section on emotional pain would help with addictions - I'm a smoker! The problem is that I don›t really have a strong desire to quit smoking, but I know for health reasons it would be best to so!

Also, the main reason I bought the pkg was for the section on healing teeth & gums, which seems to be helping! I've since noticed that you have a full pkg available just for the teeth & gums, is the pkg that I bought sufficient to heal my teeth... or do I need to buy this specific pkg?

I've been really enjoying the sessions; I find them quick & easy to follow!

I really appreciate your work!

Thank you,

C

I have just listened to the audio of Money Issues with Dawn Crystal and I found it very therapeutic and given me a sense of relaxation.

Please convey this message to Dawn for me and Mahalo for the much loved session.

Regards,

J

I'm so happy and grateful to have met Dawn Crystal. I find her energy and joy contagious. I've worked with Dawn for 6 months and so much has cleared from my mind and body. She is a healing blessing to me.

Thank you, thank you, Dawn. I am so thrilled.

G

WOW! I woke up this morning thinking about you and your incredible work that you do. I had a private session with you about a year ago. It was only 30 minutes, but it was without a doubt very, very powerful. It made me a believer in what you do, I was a total skeptic before the session. Not now, I knew within 24 hours after our session that something was shifting, physically, in a good way. Unfortunately, I didn't keep up with listening to the MP3's that were included in the package that I purchased and now I'm back to where I started. The package was purchased from Eram Saeed's webcast called From Heartache to Joy. FHTJ.com. I truly wish that I had recorded our session so that I could replay it over and over. Dawn, you're a remarkable woman. Thank you for changing my life for the better! I pray that you are showered with Blessings everyday of your life You certainly deserve it! P.S. I have no affiliation with Eram Saeed whatsoever.

J

Hi Dawn, This is me, dancing with Joy. I had deliberately waited to get my Pupp's bloodwork repeated to give his Healing time to process. I Knew we would get Good News and we Did! His white blood cell count & lymphocytes are Normal! His blood platlet count went from 75,000/80,000 (low) to 305,000, gloriously Normal! It feels to me that our bond together has deepened as well.

My hip and lower back pain are Gone! I have now found an affordable Handiman that I believe will do a great job, allowing me to (finally!) put my home on the market. The fatigue persists, which makes me wonder what Lesson I have yet to learn or remember, or, what past Life issue may be raising up for healing. I may be making another appointment with you.

Your humbleness, clear Intent and Focus on Only that which is to the Highest, Greatest Good, and determination that no ego only Source is what is are Inspiring and humbling. I So Appreciate and am Grateful to you and Source. I hope your Pupp's leg is All Better! Congratulations on & many Blessings in your new Home!

From Zorro & my Hearts to Yours,

Thank you! Thank you! Thank you!

Love, B

Last year I purchased Dawn Crystal's Anti-Aging set of mp3s from Your Wealth Revolution and a 30-minute phone session was also included. I was able to talk to Dawn in early September, and although I mainly wanted to ask about help for weight gain, I'm glad I mentioned to her that I experienced a kind of numbness and ache in my left arm when lying down. It was probably something impeding the circulation, but using her special sounds and breath work, Dawn worked on the problem, and later that night when I went to sleep, I noticed that there was a definite improvement. Subsequently the symptoms disappeared. I don't know how serious the issue was but I'm grateful for being able to receive my first live healing.

Thanks a lot. Wish you all the best!

V

Hi Dawn,

I have a question about purchasing your healing mp3s. I'm new to purchasing these and wanted to know what the process is once you buy online. Do you receive the link or files through email and are you able to download them onto an iPhone or iPad?

My mom and I have recently discovered you and have experienced so much healing already. My deep appreciation for the work you do.

Thank you in advance for your help,

H

I have sought out and have paid so many sound healers and nothing shifted for me.

Until I heard a radio show Dawn Crystal was doing. Something shifted for me by just listening to the replay of this radio show. Dawn Crystal is the real deal and definitely sent to us by the

Divine. I booked a session, I was somewhat skeptical, but my intuition said do it, loud and clear.

It was amazing. Dawn shared that the process would be working for a while after my session. It's been two weeks today and I have not felt this joyous and free in 20 years. Give yourself the best gift ever, work with Dawn Crystal, I will continue to work with her as long as she is doing this work.

Bless you Dawn. Your healing is a miracle.

M

~~~

Dear Crystal,

I am deeply grateful to you for the healing that you gave to me this past Saturday. While I have been working for the last 6 months on relationship issues in this lifetime and healing the many soul contracts I have had with my father, husbands and men in my life, as well as female authoritarians, I have only recently been touching on my own feminine issues and relationships with women.

I was aware that the sadness and loss of not being loved was still in me, and aware that not being loved was both a genetic line issue and a soul contract that I had made in for this lifetime, I was not aware of my issues related to my abortion nor was I aware that his Soul was still present in my body. Didn't even know that was possible.

Following my healing, when I went to bed, my uterus started contracting as though I were giving birth. Given that I was sleep deprived from all the individual work I had done for the previous two weeks, I took a homeopathic remedy for muscle spasms and wounds. It immediately relaxed and I slept for 10 hours.

The next day, I woke up experiencing a lot of grief. A friend, who is psychic, came over and saw the Soul and identified him as a loving, active boy. We had a discussion and she offered that I needed to welcome him back into my womb and release him to Creator. I did that three times.

This morning I lit a candle to honour him and send him on his way. I now feel at peace and ready to move on to the next issue that arose in my dreams.

I am deeply grateful to you for helping me take one more step on my road to healing wherever it leads me.

Blessings to you and your work,

S

I lost my back right third molar, more than ten years ago while eating corn nuts. I couldn't tell what tooth was and what was corn nut at the time. OMG. With Great hope I bought Dawn Crystal's Dental Care package. MY TOOTH GREW BACK!!!! It's once rough, jagged edges smooth now as a normal tooth should be! What Just Happened!?? THANK YOU Dawn!! You Are a Rock Star in sound healing m'dear!! TY TY TY TY TY!!!!

K

Dear Dawn,

"Miraculous" is the word that keeps coming to mind as every day brings the Joy of discovering something else that has been Transformed. And each return to Balance feels as natural as Breathing!

I feel like I have come back to Life, Lighter & more Present with myself.

A back injury... Healed! No more pain! I had listened to the Joint segment of Total Body Rejuvination ONCE and my hips are remarkably better. I discovered this as my Pupp & I were hiking in the park & I Felt So Much More Comfortable!

I was brushing my teeth when I realized that the tooth pain was Gone! We had worked on "fear" for literally a few minutes and, the next time something "scary" had happened - I Felt Calm, and the phrase that popped into my head was, "I Am Strong!", and, I Felt that!

And the Messages you gave me from my Beautiful Daughter who had passed a month before our Private Session have Transformed my Life! Yes, there are times I cry, times I would like to text or call her, of course! But now, the predominate feeling is one of Joy, of Relief - She Really IS OK! More than "OK", she Is Filled with Joy & Peace & Love, & is having a Grand Adventure in her New Life! I "knew" that before, now, I Really Know it!

There's more too, but, I think the above conveys that Dawn Crystal IS the Real Deal! What it may not convey is your Authenticity, your genuine Compassion, and the Nonjudgemental, Caring ways you interact with those of us Blessed with meeting you and being Transformed through through your Gifts. I am So Grateful for the Wonderfull Changes you have, and still are, through your recordings, bringing about in my Life.

Thank You Dawn Crystal. Many Blessings to You!

Love,

B

Dear Dawn Crystal,

Your sessions are a great help for me, a very positive transformation is going on!

I always believed in the healing capacities of sound, and now you give me the opportunity to discover by your beautiful and powerful voice the incredible benefits of it.

I am very grateful for this magnificent present I received from you!

Thank you so much!

You changed my life!

Love,

A

Hello Dawn,

Yes I would love to write you a testimonial!

I always feel at a loss for words just as the healing you do is beyond words. It is in the etheric and energetic realms that then transform into the physical. I feel more energy, liveliness, sparkle, and joy in life.

K

Hi Dawn & or Dawn's team!

I'm a bit of an energetic being so I will do my best to put some of my experiences into words. You may need to pick out chunks for a testimonial. and I this is not at all coherent its OK to delete it!

I found Dawn through Learning Strategies. I was on the 1st series she did. I would have been on more, but somehow I didn't know she did more than one. It was wonderful. I had hip pain when I slept, and the 1st time I listened while I was listening my hip pain went away. That blew me away! I listened to them intermittently and enjoyed it. It made a huge shift in my relationship with my husband. I used it to clear issues with my dog. I do a lot of other energy clearing stuff, so I got sidetrack. I was always curious but never ambitions enough to look up Dawn on the Internet until about February. I was out on a bike trail with the dogs & slipped on ice & broke my leg. I had a lot of down time, so I looked her up. I was looking online for a private session. On like how did I create this how can I uncreate this what else is possible? And what can I clear so it doesn't happen in the future? That kinda looked like a dead-end street, but I signed up for her email.

So, with the Total Body Rejuvenation I kept listening to the Ankle one a lot. I do think it has helped the healing process. I have also listened to the teeth one & that has been great. I've unfortunately had a lot of dental work a & had to have 2 crowns this winter as well & it has been wonderful!

I got the new dental package as well & the coolest thing about that is that my teeth feel cleaner after I listen to it. I also had a tooth that had a fill that hurts & it hurts a lot less now. I still can't floss behind it, but I have started chewing on that side of my mouth.

I have no desire to get sick but if I do I know I can out one of your mp3's on & clear it which is phenomenal!

Do you of have you considered doing something on sleep? My husband has problems sleeping.

Thank you for being you & in the world & on the planet ( yes possibly the same thing). Thank you for being as weird & won-derful as you are and using your gifts & talents to contribute to the world.

And finally, I just have to say this is really weird. This is probably the longest email I've written ever.

Thank you

M.

Dear Friends,

I participated on a free online course with Siegfried. I'm sorry I can't recall all her name, yet it was a gift indeed as she introduced Dawn amongst many guests.

Dawn was one of two who touched me very deeply in a short video where she used her ' sounding '.

This went so deep as if an invisible hand was reaching inside me and lifting out what was ripe to be released, in my case emotional pain.

Sound has always been a close friend of mine though strangely i can't listen to much music these days.

Dawn's sound expression though had a wholly new expression, very pure and liberating. I could feel her journey that she shared as this gift was given to her.

I would want everyone to be free from pain and know that Dawn will be able to assist humanity to a new place of freedom.

Thank you.

J.

I always feel at a loss for words just as the healing you do is beyond words. It is in the etheric and energetic realms that then transform into the physical. I feel more energy, liveliness, sparkle, and joy in life.

K.

Dawn Crystal's Anti-Aging and Total Body Rejuvenation sound healing PDFs feel miraculous! A literal Godsend.

I only wish they could be used without headphones from a CD or cassette for less EMF radiation. (Cannot be used without WiFi/cellular connection.) Would use more often this way.

Thank you, Dawn Crystal, for sharing your spectacular gifts!

D.

# ABOUT THE AUTHOR

**Dawn Crystal**, an internationally recognized Voice Sound Healer, Body-mind Intuitive, respected Intuitive Life Coach, Soul Reader, Medium, Pain Release Expert and Best-selling Author (*PAIN FREE Made Crystal Clear!*), is known as a **LEADING TRANSFORMATIONAL EXPERT** incorporating ancient wisdom for modern day success.

**Dawn is passionate about helping people** clear emotional and physical blockages, so they can manifest from their higher selves, step into their full potential, and lead their lives and businesses in ways that align effectively with their souls› purpose.

**Dawn helps her clients to release themselves quickly from pain**, emotional and physical, and she is an active mentor for entrepreneurs, CEO's, and celebrities, helping everyone! Dawn is the "go-to" person to get out of pain fast, in minutes!

**Dawn participates regularly on global teleseminars**, radio shows and podcasts. Dawn was recently interviewed by the *Today Show, Dr. Oz, Rachel Ray, The View,* etc. Dawn hosts her own radio show, *Pain Free Fast & Easy!* on the News for the Soul Network. For the past two years she has done a live bi-weekly program at

Learning Strategies Corporation of Minneapolis called, "Sound Healing / Silent Clearing."

**Dawn's unique sound healing CD has been purchased by clients around the globe, and she is available on both phone and Skype, as well as for teleseminars.**

Dawn lives a peaceful life on Maui, along with her adorable dog, Hoku.

This is Dawn's sixth book in her Made Crystal Clear series: *PAIN FREE, FATIGUE FREE, FEAR FREE, HAPPINESS, PET TALK, ABUNDANCE,* each published by Outskirts Press, available in paperback and ebook formats from Outskirts Press (outskirtspress.com) and from Amazon (amazon.com) and from Barnes & Noble (bn.com).

"I wouldn't change anything about my life; it's a gift," she affirms, and she transmits this inner strength to those she works with, giving them a grounding, a stable psychological place abounding with safety and love.

"I wouldn't do it over again, but I am glad where I ended up."

To see a ten-minute interview video with Dawn Crystal, go to

https://tinyurl.com/ybg3osgp .

To see almost 100 videos featuring Dawn Crystal, go to

https://www.youtube.com/channel/
UCTVOeWAA5eI0_5T4Eagcn7Q/videos

# REVIEW ABUNDANCE?

Book reviews help readers and authors connect. They are very valuable. Writing one is an act of generosity.

Amazon.com sells more than half the books purchased yearly in the U.S., and their book reviews are highly influential.

Consider reviewing *ABUNDANCE Made Crystal Clear* at amazon.com or elsewhere. This will be appreciated by the author and her potential readers.